EVERY.
BODY.
BEAUTIFUL.

If she's beautiful, does
that mean you're not?

NATALIE CAREY

www.barbellblondie.com

This book is dedicated to the collection of strong women I know who make me reach farther, stand up taller, and speak louder.

And to Mak, for making me feel beautiful and loved every day that I've known you.

CONTENTS

Chapter One
The Best Friggin' Day Ever

I ONCE ATE a whole box of cookies knowing I was going to throw them up afterwards. I airbrushed a picture of myself in college to look thinner. I spent years sucking in my stomach to look skinnier and wondered why I had digestive problems. I wore low cut shirts to nightclubs and parties that made me feel vulnerable and exposed only because people told me I had great tits and should show them off. I slept with guys too soon and often because I thought I was lucky to even have them pay attention to a chubby plain girl like me.

I spent nearly half a lifetime disliking what I looked like. I'm not writing this book because I'm the only one who feels this way. I'm writing this because after I started admitting these things to people, I realized a lot of women have felt this way at one point or another in varying degrees. We spend years comparing our bodies and our looks to other women and trying to please the people we want to attract to us by altering our looks. I am one of many women who has struggled with an eating disorder of some kind, but for me, the disordered eating was one of many symptoms of hating the way I looked.

I don't want others to go through their lives repeating these actions and feeling bad about themselves when there are solutions available. I want to share my message and ignite positive body image as a catalyst towards a world where women feel more beautiful and content with themselves. Body image is how you feel about yourself and the way you look. If you have positive body image, you feel good about yourself and like the way you look. If you have negative body image than you probably don't like the way you look or who you are, and may compare yourself to others you consider to be a better standard of beauty.

Our looks matter. To pretend they don't matter would be naïve of me. It wouldn't be truthful either to claim that our outward appearance would stop mattering to others if we just loved ourselves enough. But I am a firm believer that the entirety of a person is what attracts others, and it's time for women to strengthen their confidence and claim ownership of who they are, both physically and inwardly.

It's so easy to dislike the way you look, especially as a woman. I know many men struggle with this as well, but I don't feel I know enough the male's perspective to speak to it. If you pay attention, you'll start to notice that categorizing women's looks is something our society does constantly, in almost every medium, and that this way of thinking is drilled into us from a young age. We are told what celebrities are hot or not, and shown that one bad day on the red carpet will earn you years of criticism. Female celebrities are congratulated on getting their pre-baby bodies back. Magazines shout at us from their covers to get flatter abs and learn better makeup tips and to do our hair in new sexy styles. Songs saluting attractive women with specific assets play on our radios and mobile devices. Social media that features sexy attractive women typically gets more attention than almost *anything else* on the internet. We cut ourselves down, judge other women's looks, compare tiny details. I strive to be more conscientious of measuring myself and others by these impossible standards, as I'm sure many of you do, but when it constantly surrounds us, we seldom realize how ingrained it is.

It's everywhere.

No wonder so many women feel terrible about the way they look.

Why don't we value inner beauty and its potential to radiate as much as our external features? I can almost feel the eye rolls as I bring up inner beauty, but it is more important than we are giving it credit for being. I think the phrase inner beauty is something people sometimes say to describe a person who is considered unattractive, but this usage bothers me. Inner beauty is the energy that a person radiates through their kindness, happiness, goodness of heart, and treatment of others. If you know someone who has a lot of inner beauty, you'll notice that their beauty radiates out of them and onto everyone around them. Their smile and warmth light up a room and make people around them feel good. They glow, and you'll find yourself being attracted to their magnetism without thinking twice about their physical features.

I have a theory: that if every woman in the world realized how uniquely beautiful, strong, and significant she was, that so many things would instantaneously get better. Imagine if every girl and woman in the world saw that they are beautiful because of who they are and what they are capable of, if they realized their worth, stuck up for themselves and others, and refused to be depreciated by what the world has been trying to make us believe, that we are nothing if we are not good looking. Imagine if we put as much emphasis on working on our inner beauty as we did focusing on what we look like. If we stopped spending our time and money on makeup and beauty gadgets and body alterations and instead dedicated what we saved towards enriching our lives and interests and passions and love. How incredible would that be, if every woman on earth realized her own unique beauty, and the world became a more wonderful and authentic and accepting place? Imagine how much power women would have as a collective, if each of us knew our worth! Imagine how much goodness would arise out of that on a global scale!

I can imagine it. It would be amazing.

It would be the best friggin' day ever.

I envision a world where we spend more energy thinking about three things:

1) **Focus on cultivating inner beauty.** Figure out what makes you happy, and how to bring joy to others. Treat yourself and those around you with kindness and compassion and honesty.

2) **Enrich yourself by taking care of your health, fitness, and nutrition.** Worry more about how your body feels and what it is capable of versus whether you measure up to someone else's standard of beauty. Fuel yourself with good food, healthy habits, and movement instead of "likes" and compliments on your social media.

3) **Recognize how beautiful you are.** Combining inner beauty and a healthy body results in one seriously beautiful human. Cultivate this for yourself, and recognize how valuable you are.

I wish that vision was a reality, so I am going to do everything I can within this book to help you realize your inner and outer beauty, and to recognize how truly lovely you are. The great thing about body image is that we can shift, transform, and influence it to be positive and strong, and that is what I wish for you.

Having worked in the health and fitness industry since 2011, many of my daily conversations revolve around feeling better about ourselves. This is an incredibly large issue for so many of us, and I don't know why I continue to be shocked that nearly every woman I speak with has had battles with how she feels about herself. Why are so many women struggling to feel good about themselves and thinking they are alone in that battle? It doesn't have to be that way. We need more positive body image, and we need it yesterday. We are going to create a revolution of women who feel good about themselves and know they are beautiful and valuable.

It all starts with you.

EVERY. BODY. BEAUTIFUL.

2006: This was our senior year in college at the quarterly Undie
Run during finals week. I Photoshopped my stomach in this picture,
because I hated standing next to my friend's perfectly muscular
abs. I was so embarrassed of the negligible amount of cellulite on
my tummy and didn't want any memories of imperfection.

Now when I look at this picture, instead of remembering the absolute blast we had, I only focus on the area I know I Photoshopped, wondering if anyone else can spot it. I thought the alteration would improve my memory of the moment, but it ironically did the opposite.

2004: My best friend and me at our favorite fraternity party of the year. We were supposed to be as colorful as possible, so I resourcefully cut up an old T-shirt into a series of strings to expose all the cleavage I could. I remember feeling very uncomfortable all night, with people staring at my chest, but thought I had to dress this way to get attention from guys.

EVERY. BODY. BEAUTIFUL.

"How beautiful would it be if we could just see souls instead of bodies? To see love and compassion instead of curves."

—Karen Quan, *Write Like No One is Reading 2*

Chapter Two
I Used To Think I Was Pretty

I USED TO think I was pretty.

When I was young, I would actually sit in front of the mirror and admire things about myself that I thought were beautiful. My favorite feature was my eyebrows. I thought to myself "one day the world is going to realize how perfect my eyebrows are!" I distinctly remember thinking that everything would fall into place for me if the world could only see my perfect eyebrows that didn't need plucking! How I got it into my head that my eyebrows would help me conquer the world, I'll never know.

Me at age 11, with my flawless eyebrows and highly advanced makeup skills, striking model poses in our living room.

I don't remember comparing myself negatively to women on television or my friends or my dolls, I simply loved how I looked. When I started wearing a training bra in fourth grade, I would put on tight shirts and push my mini boobs up as high as I could, put on my mom's free lipstick samples, and strut around our apartment in her high heels, feeling like the most gorgeous woman in the universe.

I thought I was beautiful, and when I think about it, there's no reason any other child couldn't just make this assumption. I think my parents told me I was beautiful the way supportive parents do, but this perception came entirely from a belief I had about myself.

I remember distinct occasions when my mom would indulge me and let me pose with our camera. She would play with my hair, or let me dress up in makeup and clothes, and take pictures of me staring off dreamily into the corner of exotic locations like, the living room, or our front lawn. I thought I was special and unique and talented and capable of anything. I believed in myself.

EVERY. BODY. BEAUTIFUL.

I get it from my mama...

Here's my mom hitting a glamorous pose in our living room.
Apparently, I was not the only one modeling around our house!

This was before the days of social media and reality television, when my standard of beauty was defined by the female stars of the TV shows I watched, who were all energetic, happy, funny actresses that I looked up to.

I continued to feel beautiful until I was in eighth grade, when, one day, a boy whom I considered a friend told me I was plain. "Your best friend is beautiful," he casually tossed at me, "but you're just plain."

Now, part of this was true. My junior high best friend was very beautiful, and still is to this day. But why did her unique beauty have to set the standard for how I looked? Why did her being beautiful mean that I was not?

With one sentence, my thirteen year old world exploded. With a single word he told me I was ordinary and unexceptional, and partially because the thought took me by surprise, I believed him.

I stood there, frozen, not sure quite what to say.

I'm just plain looking.

Other people don't think I'm beautiful.

I'm so stupid and delusional for thinking I was pretty.

I can't explain how or why his comment made such an impact on me. I'm sure there was something else at play that day, to take such a huge toll on what had been a lifetime of high self-esteem. Maybe I had a crush on him or also thought my friend was more attractive than me. I was in those awkward teenage years, and was probably starting to feel a little unsteady. I don't remember. I think it was also the feeling of stupidity, that perhaps the thing I had thought true all of these years was wrong.

EVERY. BODY. BEAUTIFUL.

1998: Me and the boy who told me I was plain. Yes, that's his actual face. And yes, that's my actual face, too.

What I do know is that I had lived for thirteen years thinking I was beautiful, but what this boy destroyed in one sentence would take me two decades to rebuild. No compliment or reassurance could undo what that one poisonous comment did when it dug into my brain and latched on. "You're just plain" would repeat in my head anytime someone paid me a compliment or mentioned they thought another girl was pretty. I would even repeat it to others sometimes, telling them how ordinary I was, as if admitting to my plain-ness was empowering. I also started getting the comment "at least you're proportional" any time I would discuss my body issues, which is one of the worst things you can say to a college girl lacking confidence. "Proportional" was another way of saying "equal chub distributed around your body but not quite fat," and that one clanged around in my head too.

I would spend high school, college, and most of my 20's feeling like I was average. I had pretty low standards for the men I dated and how they treated me. I always felt like I was lucky enough to even have a date in the first place, like they had taken pity on me or something, and I let guys treat me like I was nothing. I always thought each guy was my last chance at a relationship, because nobody would want the plain proportional girl.

Pretty fucked up.

Have you ever felt that way?

Maybe you have. Maybe you still do.

Two decades later, I finally managed to coax out the beautiful self-assured person that had been hiding for so many years. I think this person is in all of us, and that the more confident you feel about yourself and your body, the more beautiful you become. I want the same revolutionary experience for every woman out there who has ever doubted her self-worth for even one second because she didn't look a certain way or fit someone else's standards. Being beautiful is not a zero-sum game, there is enough exceptionalism in all of us to go around. Just because your best friend, or that model in the magazine, or the woman across the bar from you happens to be attractive, it doesn't mean that you can't be hot and sexy and awesome and magical as well. Beauty is not one thing and none of the others.

EVERY. BODY. BEAUTIFUL.

Holding on to this grudge that never fully healed wasted a lot of my energy, but it eventually evolved into fuel to communicate these feelings of being worth less that I know so many others share with me. Recently, after making peace with my looks and my body, and sometimes even having the audacity to tell myself I'm beautiful, I decided to forgive this junior high boy. While what he said was harsh, I cringe to think of the things I may have said to others as an inconsiderate young girl. I honestly do not think he meant his comment maliciously, and was probably just repeating some phrase he'd heard somewhere.

I wish I could talk to that thirteen year old girl and give her a hug. I would tell her that she is beautiful, but I would also remind her that it's important to be humble and kind. I would tell her that how she feels about herself is entirely up to her, and to find the things that make her feel beautiful and latch on fiercely to them. To appreciate the people who appreciate her. To not let one teenage boy mess with her head and make her think she's worth less than any other woman. I would tell her she's fucking gorgeous.

"Happiness and confidence are the prettiest things you can wear."

—Taylor Swift

Chapter Three
Take Action

I WORK TOWARDS a positive body image every day, and yes, it is work. Now, I want to help others feel better about themselves. Every revolution requires taking action, and by putting into motion the following items, you can make progress towards feeling better about yourself and loving what you've got!

+Get Moving

Movement has so many health benefits, but to appreciate your body fully, you've got to use it and see what it can do!

Many women tend to feel more beautiful and better about themselves when they feel strong, so see if this also works for you. You will also feel better if your body feels better, which happens to be a side effect of movement and exercise. Once you get moving, you won't be able to help but realize how awesome you are and appreciate yourself.

Every woman I spoke to or who shared their story with me while writing this book told me how influential movement was in helping them gain positive body image. The phrase "I feel beautiful when I feel strong" was said so many times to me, and every time I was more surprised, because I thought I was the only one who felt this way.

Find a form of movement that you enjoy. Here are suggestions of activities you can try, and hopefully your community offers opportunities for you to participate in at least one of them. Try one of these. Try all of these. Go down the list until you find something you like and then stick with it. The more you feel your body move, flow, sweat, ache, stretch, reach, and do what it was meant to do, the more you will feel beautiful and proud of how you feel and look:

EVERY. BODY. BEAUTIFUL.

- Basketball
- Biking
- Bowling
- Climbing stairs
- Dance
- Elliptical
- Field hockey
- Flag football
- Football
- Frisbee
- Golf
- Gymnastics
- Hiking
- Hockey
- Home workout videos
- Horseback riding
- House work
- Hula hooping
- Ice skating
- Jogging
- Jump rope
- Karate
- Kayaking
- Line dancing
- Martial arts
- Pilates
- Racquetball
- Rock climbing
- Roller-skating
- Rowing
- Run 5K/Half/Full Marathon
- Shovel snow
- Skateboarding
- Skating
- Skiing/Snowboarding
- Soccer
- Spin class
- Stretching
- Surfing
- Swimming
- Tap dancing
- Tennis
- Volleyball
- Walking
- Walking the dog
- Washing the Car
- Weight lifting
- Yard work
- Yoga
- Zumba class

+Set a Goal

My recommendation is to set a body goal that is not appearance oriented. Those kinds of goals tend to be difficult to measure, and can be disheartening if you feel like you haven't achieved them. Instead, set goals that make you focus on getting your body stronger and feeling capable. Your goal could be to run a 5k, take a yoga class every week for a month, perform a cartwheel, or squat your bodyweight. It can be anything you want, as long as it is measurable and attainable. Pick a goal that is realistic enough that you think you could do it with some effort, but that is also challenging enough that you haven't tried it yet. Even better, once you achieve that goal, like I know you are going to do, imagine how great *that* will feel?

I think many goals are centered around a number on the bathroom scale, and in some instances I see merit in that, but if you really want to feel good, then set a goal that won't solely be reflected on the scale. Some goals you might set for yourself:

> - Be able to walk or run a certain distance, even one mile
> - Keep up with your kids on the playground
> - Avoid alcohol during the week
> - Quit processed sugar for a whole month
> - Start a monthly hiking group with friends
> - Keep a workout diary
> - Run a marathon
> - Do an obstacle race
> - Take a dance class

EVERY. BODY. BEAUTIFUL.

2016: This was me in the best shape of my life. I ate precisely what was on my nutrition plan, rehearsed at the studio five to six times a week without fail, and was trying to get my body fat as low as possible so that I would have less weight to throw around the pole in this exhausting routine. (Photography credit: George Grigorian)

There are so many goals whose achievement will make you feel incredible that the scale will not be able to reflect. Scales are important, but they cannot provide an accurate measurement of your worth as a human.

+Eating Well

Eat well to feel well. Whether it comes from feeling a certain amount of shame around eating foods that we know aren't very good for us, or because those foods usually don't make us feel good physically after ingesting them, it's always a good idea to eat well and fuel your body with wholesome healthy food.

This doesn't mean that indulging in treats in moderation is out of the question. I'm saying that eating fast food and junk all day doesn't make your body feel good, and then you don't feel great about yourself. Eating nutritious food is like creating a fountain of youth within yourself! You can give your body the nutrients it needs to do what it does best, and you'll feel energized, fueled, and satisfied.

I like to eat really well during the week, and splurge a little on the weekends. The healthier you eat, the better you'll feel, but we are human and sometimes need to indulge in gummy bears and burgers. Or any weird combination of rich foods you enjoy!

+Take Care of your Beautiful Self

Taking care of ourselves encompasses so much. Care can range from going to the doctor to having a symptom checked out, to getting a massage, to investing in good skin care and sunscreen. When you take better care of the body you are blessed with, it will take better care of you.

Drinking water, getting enough sleep, stretching, taking vitamins, laughing, and managing your health care means taking pride in your body, because it's the only one you're going to get, so do whatever you can to preserve it.

Taking care of yourself also means surrounding yourself with people who have your back, or in other words, humans that you should think of as your tribe. These are the people who want good things for you, who appreciate all that you offer, who will help to fortify this strong belief that you are loved and respected. Sometimes finding your tribe can be hard, and they probably won't all be found in the same place. It means that to find these people who will take care of you, you have to take care of them too. It means you must search for others who have inner beauty and radiate positivity and kindness. You should recognize that in them and appreciate their worth.

Do not waste time with people who leave you feeling drained and bad about yourself. These people have not worked on their inner beauty yet, and they're not eligible for your tribe right now. Take care of your beautiful self and spend as much time as possible with the tribe of wonderfully quirky and awesomely imperfect people you love you as much as you adore them.

+Mirror Talk

Ah, mirrors. Love them or hate them, you inevitably have an opinion about yourself when you look into one. Unfortunately, I think a lot of women look into a mirror and pick out what they think is flawed with themselves. If you are thinking something negative about yourself every time you look into the mirror, consider how much that will add up over time. Negative thoughts become a habit, just like anything else that we repeat over and over. Whatever you tell yourself shapes how your brain works. If you constantly tell yourself you look fat, or this one part of you has cellulite, or if only this one thing was bigger or smaller, you are reinforcing that negative body image and damaging your confidence on a daily basis.

Our brains are powerful things, but they are also impressionable. Our brains don't always know the difference between visions, affirmations, dreams, and reality. If we constantly inform our brain that we feel bad about ourselves, it doesn't know that's just an opinion and will accept it as truth. Luckily, if we focus on telling our brain positive thoughts, it will assume that's the truth.

Instead, every time you look into the mirror, point out one trait, physical or otherwise, that you like about yourself, and if you can, say it out loud! Finding things you like about yourself and focusing on those may help to increase your positive body image and how you feel about yourself. Compliments don't just have to come from other people; you can pay yourself as many compliments as you like, especially if you are *feelin' yo'self!* You can even place sticky notes on the mirror to remind you and reinforce the beauty you want to feel. Check out my 100 in 10 List coming up later in this chapter to see all the things I notice about myself that I like to get inspired for your own self-compliments.

If you're having trouble looking into the mirror and finding something you want to compliment yourself on, fake it!

+Awesome Activities

Most of us who want to be healthy have concerns about how a healthy lifestyle will fit into our social life. So many activities these days are focused around booze centered activities and junk food. A lot of my clients worry that they'll have to choose between their social life and looking and feeling the way they want to, but this doesn't have to be true! Success and balance is all about getting creative and focusing on your relationships more than the calories you're consuming.

I've started to plan get-togethers around healthy activities so that I get to see my friends and also feel good about myself. I'll schedule hikes, fitness classes, trips to the beach, grocery-shopping trips, and even threw a smoothie making party in order to combine health and socializing. As soon as I stopped thinking I had to be alone on my journey to enjoy life and my body, I realized the possibilities were endless for activities that would bring me closer to my friends and make me feel great. Here are some suggestions to keep you and your social life happy and healthy:

❖ **Crockpot Date Night:** My boyfriend and I will throw ingredients into the crockpot, head out for a fun activity like go kart racing, a workout, or people watching, and when we come home we've got a healthy meal waiting for us with minimal effort.

❖ **Smoothie Brunch:** My roommates and I happen to own 4 different blending apparatuses, so I bought a bunch of blend-able ingredients, invited a ton of people over, and we tried to come up with new and different smoothie recipes. People ended up dividing into teams and working together on creations.

❖ **Rock Climbing and Coffee:** Awhile back I wanted to try a bunch of new sports, like rock climbing, Crossfit, and modern dance. I would meet up with a friend, try an intro class, and grab coffee afterwards while we talked about life and whether we enjoyed the new activity or not. Coffee or tea dates in general are one of my favorite ways to spend time with people, additional activity or not.

❖ **Buddy Errands**: We all have to run errands, so why not run them together? Groceries, home improvement, and shopping can all be way more fun with other friends who are busy or on the go. This is a great last minute weekend hangout to help you enjoy every second you have out of the office with cool people while still taking care of your never ending todo list.

❖ **Local Events:** Get out of your comfort zone and look around you. If you think outside the box, most communities offer a variety of great activities that don't involve eating poorly. Outdoor movies, museum exhibits, volunteer opportunities, festivals, and sporting events are all things that don't require you to eat or drink to participate. Get brave and try something you've never done before, support local artists whose shows you've never heard of, and see what's going on around you. You don't have to love the new activity, but at the very least it will give you some time to grow your relationships in a healthy way that will expand your experiences.

❖ **Park and Chill**: Grab a blanket, your sunscreen, water, healthy snacks, and your board games or cards, and head to the nearest park, beach, lake, or backyard. Laugh with friends, get a tan, and enjoy the outdoors. This is one of my favorite activities that everyone can participate in no matter your fitness goals!

❖ **The Standards:** If you want to go to a bar or food related event because you don't want to have to change your lifestyle completely, there's totally a way to do it. Order waters, seltzers with lime, or low sugar liquors while you're out and keep your weekly drink intake low. Alcohol can affect how your body and mind feel for days afterwards, so be mindful. If you're headed to a restaurant that offers less than healthy fare because you are obligated or simply want to go with friends, consider looking at the menu beforehand and figuring out either what you can order or modify on the menu that will make you feel great during and after!

I threw a Smoothies and Bubbles party for my friends and clients that was so much fun! We made all kinds of smoothies like Chocolate Avocado, Key Lemon Pie (waffle included!), and Strawberry Shortcake. I had healthy options as well as champagne for people who wanted to drink a little. Win-win for everyone!

+Discover Your Fashion Style

One of the final steps I took to really feel great about myself was to think about what style made me the most beautiful. I think positive body image and increased self-worth start from the inside and work their way out, and I truly think that beauty shines from within people, but if I'm being completely honest, what really solidified this whole process was polishing it all off with developing a style that made me feel great.

1) Start to notice "looks." Think about what styles, colors, and fabrics look great on you or that you are naturally drawn to. You can use fashion bloggers, friends, designers, and even art to draw inspiration from. What "look" makes you feel strong and beautiful?

2) As you realize you like certain looks, ask if any of these styles sound most like your personality, what you want to represent, and what you want to project. My own style is sparkly and edgy with just a little bit of bubblegum in there. Try making a Pinterest board or an album of screenshots of styles you like.

3) Have some friends help you go through your closet and get rid of items you don't want to keep. Don't just toss out jeans that don't fit anymore, lose the jeans that you don't absolutely love, or the ones that are out of style. Donating them to a charitable organization is always a great option!

4) Have those same friends, or at the very least, your smartphone, (which you know is your best friend anyways), go to 2-4 stores to find standards for your new look. I recommend reading *The One Hundred* by Nina Garcia, to help figure out the classic standbys.

5) Take photos of yourself in all the things you try on. If you have to wonder if you love it, you

probably don't. Clothing that you are meant to buy makes you feel like a queen. Pick the items that you feel great in that *also* look great on you in the photo. Start with buying the standards, and then build on it gradually. Your closet will be ever evolving, just like you.

When you have a wardrobe that you look great in, you *know* you look your best, so you feel your best, and you project that towards others. Then they realize you're at your best, so they will treat you as best as they can, which reinforces, affirms, and validates how you've been treating and viewing yourself. This solidifies all your work, reminds you how good you've got it, and allows you to be as awesome as you just so happen to be!

+Fake It 'Til You Make It

Confidence is one of the most beautiful traits someone can have, and people are naturally drawn to those who walk into a room with their head held high and a smile on their face. This might feel really challenging for you to pull off, but I encourage you to give it a whirl.

I try to smile at everyone I make eye contact with and hold their gaze until they either look away or smile back. When I first started doing this, it was so intimidating to me, but I would force that eye contact and smile, and it was pretty awesome to see how others would respond to me. The more you practice this, the more natural it will feel, so fake this confidence until you make it. These small actions of self-assurance will draw other beautiful people towards you, and they in turn will point out your best traits. People who are attracted to this confidence, whether you struggle with it or not, are the kind of people you want in your tribe; they are the type that will look beyond outward appearance to what's happening on the inside.

Showing confidence is simple, it just sounds scary. Be yourself, be genuine, say what's in your heart. Show qualities that reflect compassion, unconditional positive regard, and patience, and keep reminding yourself of these things every day until it feels more natural. There is a lack of these qualities in our world today, but if you can show a glimmer of them to others, you will already be ahead of the curve.

Fake it 'til you make it also works for complimenting yourself and even working out and eating healthy! You might find it hard to compliment yourself. You may feel really lazy or discouraged in your workouts. You might eat a salad and follow it up with a bar of chocolate (guilty as charged!). This process is all about taking small, constructive steps towards being a better you. If you can't think of a real compliment for yourself, say something you wish was true, and turn it into a compliment. If you wish your butt looked different, tell yourself "one day I hope I love this awesome boot-ay that I've got." When you don't feel like working out or didn't have a great exercise session, focus on the positive; "I'm going to start with a warmup and see how I feel after 10 minutes" or "I'm so lucky I got to move today!." If you started your day off eating healthy, wholesome food, but indulged in some ice cream for dessert, remind yourself "I fueled my body with great nutrients today, and tomorrow I'm going to stay focused on making choices that feel great to my body!" We can't be perfect, but we can make progress by faking it until we make it closer to our visions.

This doesn't have to feel disingenuous, just because you're trying something that doesn't exactly match how you currently feel. A lesson my dad taught me is perfect for this scenario; whenever I get angry and call him to vent, he always tells me to say a prayer for the person I'm angry at. He says that even if you don't feel like wishing them something good, pray that in the future, you hope you genuinely wish them good things. This is helpful with ex-boyfriends as well as body image. Let's say I was mad at Jake* for breaking up with me, but for my sake, I say a prayer that one day I will be at peace with the situation and be able to wish him well. It's still a positive thought, and it's still authentic. If you dislike something about your body, you can say to yourself "I really hope one day I make peace with my stretch marks." Just because you don't like something currently, you can still infuse positivity into the way you think about it, and be sincere to yourself.

*Jake is a fictitious name I made up for my imaginary boyfriend, who strongly resembles Jake Gyllenhaal. Also, Jake Gyllenhaal if you are reading this I was never really mad at you and please call me, okay?

+100 in 10 List

Whenever someone I know feels a little lost and is trying to sort themselves or their life out, I recommend

EVERY. BODY. BEAUTIFUL.

my 100 in 10 List. You can grab a pen and paper and write down 100 things you like in 10 minutes. These 100 things can be things you like about your body, things you like in general, and traits that make you who you are. The cool thing about this exercise is that ten minutes goes by really fast, so trying to think of 100 things is super hard. You end up just writing anything that pops into your head whether it makes sense at the time or not, and that's the point. When you're put under a little pressure, you have to trust your gut, let your subconscious in, and what you end up writing down might surprise you. This is a good exercise even if you can't reach 100 things within the ten minutes; it's fine if you list 99 things, or 76, or 43.

Six years ago I was living in Japan and had no idea what I was going to do when I returned back to America. I made a 100 in 10 Goal List, laughed at most of what I had written down, and then years later came across it only to discover that most of the things on the list had come true. It's funny what we don't realize we know about ourselves. I made a list of 100 in 10 things I like and make me happy while I was writing this book, and I'll share it with you as an example:

100 in 10 Things I like That Make Me Happy

1. All my parents (I have a bonus parent!)
2. As much food as I need and want
3. Barbecues
4. Being Cozy
5. Being myself
6. Being outdoors
7. Black and gold

8. Board games
9. Books
10. Bourbon
11. Brainstorming
12. Candy
13. Champagne
14. Cheeseburgers
15. Climbing things
16. Coffee drinks
17. Collaboration
18. Compliments
19. Connecting with others
20. Creating
21. Dance
22. Determination
23. Doing my own thing
24. Early morning sunrises
25. Energy
26. Exercise
27. Family
28. Feeling strong
29. Fireworks
30. Flowers
31. Friends
32. Funny/Action/Robot Movies
33. Gambling
34. Getting along with others
35. Gratitude
36. Happiness
37. Healthy foods
38. Hugs
39. Inspiration from others
40. Introspection
41. Jewelry
42. Journaling
43. Jumping
44. Kid's movies that cause happy-tears
45. Kindness
46. Late nights
47. Laughter
48. Learning
49. Leather and studs
50. Lip balm and hand lotion!
51. Lit fireplaces
52. Love
53. Mascara
54. Movement
55. Movie hopping
56. Muscles
57. My big shoulders
58. My blonde Mohawk hair
59. My boyfriend
60. My calves
61. My different colored eyes
62. My eyebrows
63. My freckles

64. My healthy skin
65. My legs
66. My short height
67. My toes that point
68. New adventures
69. Nut butter
70. Oceans and lakes
71. Others loving each other
72. People who say nice things about others
73. Pole dancing
74. Popcorn
75. Positive attitudes
76. Positivity
77. Power words
78. Protein bars
79. Puzzles
80. Reflection
81. Scented candles
82. Shiny things
83. Sleep
84. Smiles
85. Sneakers
86. Sparkles
87. Sunshine
88. Sweating from a great workout
89. Talking to strangers
90. Taking fun pictures
91. Teaching
92. That I can do the splits!
93. Therapy sessions
94. Traveling
95. Vitamins
96. Warm weather
97. Watermelon gum
98. Weed (*Shhhh*! I think some drugs are cool!)
99. Wine
100. Writing

The 100 in 10 List should include things you love about yourself, both on the inside and outside, and things you're grateful for. Other than that, there aren't any rules. Just write down whatever pops into your head.

The 100 in 10 List is about recognizing things that make you feel special and awesome. The more beauty you see in yourself, the more beauty you see in the world, and it goes around in a circle, making more and more of it. When you treat others with the love you know you are worthy of, the more that love will manifest itself.

For more ideas, resources, and activities you can do to feel great about yourself, create a healthy lifestyle, and surround yourself with positivity, visit my website www.barbellblondie.com and become a part of the community of women who believe in positive body image!

Interlude
I'll Use the Lobby
Bathroom

WHEN I WAS 19, I got a fake ID. Getting a fake ID is a very bad idea, highly illegal, and you should never, ever do it. But most of my friends had one or were older than me, and I was tired of being left behind when they went to bars, so I got one. Once acquired, the possibilities for debauchery were endless! I could stock the kitchen with enormous handles of dark rum and cheap vodka! I could gain access to swanky sounding nightclubs in Los Angeles that were either empty or so crowded I wanted to leave immediately! And I could live every young Americans' dream of experiencing Spring Break!

That's right. My friends and I booked a trip to South Beach, Miami for Spring Break our junior year. We bought countless pieces of clothing that were mostly made up of sequins and string, and devised a sleeping plan that would fit five of us into a room with one queen bed.

The problem was I had seen what Spring Break looked like. I knew everyone would be in bikinis, trying to hook up. Easy, I thought, I'll just have to get on that binge and purge diet I know everyone is doing.

Now, let the record show that in retrospect, I don't think every girl at my college had an eating disorder. Some of them worked really hard to look the way they did, and some of them were just naturally blessed, but I suspect a lot of others went to unhealthy extremes to keep up with the standards we felt we had to measure up to, like I ended up doing. At the time though, I thought everyone was secretly maintaining an eating disorder that they hadn't bothered to clue me in on, and I was tired of being left out. I knew I wouldn't be able to stop eating, so the anorexic club was not for me. But eating a LOT of food and then throwing most of it up? Maybe I could get on board with that.

I remember the first time I made myself puke. I treated myself to ice cream, which I never let myself eat, because I knew I would be getting rid of it. I waited for a time I knew my roommates wouldn't be at the apartment. I put on music in case they came home, locked the bathroom door, and stared at the toilet, wondering what to do.

I felt gross afterwards. I felt violated. Most of all, I felt stupid.

But I kept doing it. I would eat conservatively at most meals. But after meals where I felt I had gone overboard or eaten something I shouldn't, I would discreetly find a bathroom with privacy. By the time our vacation arrived, I looked pretty great. I was carrying around this big secret that I was totally ashamed of, but I looked good.

There are a lot of moments I remember from that Spring Break trip; making out with an ex-con under a lifeguard tower until sunrise on the beach; freak dancing with an off duty cop and laughing to myself about the fake ID in my pocket; pictures with my girlfriends in the beautiful turquoise waves of Miami. But I also remember one moment, after we had gone out for fast food, and I was worried I wouldn't look hot enough in my skimpy outfit. Five girls. One shared bathroom. One secret eating disorder. So I told them I had to go number two and headed down to the hotel lobby bathroom. I stared a long time into the porcelain, hating myself.

When I was done, I headed back upstairs, did pre-party shots of crappy vodka with the girls, and headed out. I told myself I felt beautiful, but I didn't believe it.

Years later, my closest friend from the trip and I revisited that wild vacation. We laughed about the stupid shit we'd done, how horrible our accommodations had been, what young fools we'd made of ourselves. Out of nowhere, she told me, "You know, I ate nothing but carrots for a month before that trip." I stared back at her "I threw up half my meals so I could fit in my bathing suit." "Wow" she said. "Why did we do that to ourselves?" she asked. "What the fuck?" she added.

I think this is an important piece of information for me to share as part of this book, but I really struggled with how to include it. For someone who has gotten pretty darn comfortable with sharing who I am, I still worried that readers would judge me, or pity me, or fixate on this one thing instead of taking away something positive from my writing. In the past, my personal experience had always seemed like it wasn't that big of a deal, so I was a little surprised when responses to my first drafts focused on this story. For me, the bigger deal seemed to be how much I disliked myself. I never considered myself eating disordered, because it felt more like a symptom of a bigger problem instead of a problem on its own. In my late teens and early twenties, if I wasn't throwing up food, I was chain smoking, or being promiscuous, or crying a lot, or trying to be perfect at everything. I knew so many young women in college that went through something similar and then moved forward. I've also known about a dozen women that have had minor to major eating disorders. Maybe I was comparing myself to other girls and women I knew who had worse eating problems and overall life challenges than I did, so I felt like I didn't need to take it as seriously. I'm not sure.

I do know that throwing up was a way to punish myself for not living up to the standards I set for myself and how I looked. I thought I was the plain girl but at least I could be thinner. I felt mediocre at everything and felt like I couldn't succeed at anything. Nothing that happened in my life during that time seemed to loan me any confidence that I was worth anything.

EVERY. BODY. BEAUTIFUL.

I'm not sure what to call my eating disorder, my dislike of my body and looks, my lack of confidence, my feelings of failure, however you want to label it, because to me it was a whole collection of disheartening experiences rolled into one, and I can't put one name to it. I feel like by not saying it was an eating disorder, that it's disowning solidarity with the women who do use that term for their own experience, and I don't want to do that because that implies judgement to me, but calling it an eating disorder doesn't feel authentic either. I talk about this experience because I don't want anyone to feel that they need go through any of this to look a certain way. Forcing your body to do unhealthy things will not make you feel respect for yourself, and you won't achieve that feeling of strength and beauty you are most likely chasing after. You are worth so much more than the credit you give yourself. I don't talk about this experience because I want people to offer me condolences. I have been through this battle, and I know what's on the other side. I am ready to share out loud the struggle to love myself because I am far enough away from it that I can speak my truth without shame.

I just wanted to take a moment and recognize that eating disorders should not be taken lightly, and I don't want to dismiss what I went through. I want to acknowledge that whatever happened was a part of me disliking my body and myself, and I want to use that to propel forward.

There will be a "they" who read this. They will feel uncomfortable. They will be the people who want to tell me I'm wrong for saying what I have said, they will remember things differently, or even some who may separate themselves from me for revealing who I am and what I think. That will be hard, but it will also be okay. I had to share these stories and thoughts because I know there are other women out there, beautiful women who have sparkles in their soul and potential and goodness in their heart, who don't realize how wonderful they are, who I desperately wish could see what I do. Those are the women this story is for.

"Beauty shouldn't be about changing yourself to achieve an ideal or be more socially acceptable. Real beauty, the interesting, truly pleasing kind, is about honoring the beauty within you and without you. It's about knowing that someone else's definition of pretty has no hold over you."

—Golda Poretsky

Chapter Four
All My Friends are Gorgeous

RECENTLY, I WAS reflecting on my female friendships, and how I truly believe every one of them is gorgeous. I've asked myself if it's because I know how beautiful they are on the inside, that it radiates to their external looks? Or are all of my friends just coincidentally very attractive? I couldn't tell you, because to me the two gel together and I can't tell the difference. I actually believe so many of the women in my life are as attractive as the celebrities that walk the red carpet, and it made me wonder if they could see that about themselves.

I tend to attract a lot more female personal training clients than men. It might be because my company name, Barbell Blondie Athletics, has been referred to as "cute" and "feminine," so perhaps it doesn't attract males as much. After years of personal training, I have also observed that trainers tend to attract clients that are similar to them in looks, personality, goals, and mindset, so I find that my clients often share a lot of my own personal traits. Whatever the reason, I end up training mostly women, which I enjoy very much, because I understand women a little better than I understand men, and I also relate to the unique struggles that other ladies deal with because I've dealt with them myself.

Something that I've heard from many of my female clients, over and over again, but never from my male clients, is that they don't like themselves, or the way they look. Men will make requests like "help me lose my gut" or "could we make my shoulders bigger?", but women talk more about how their body makes them feel:

I'm sick of feeling uncomfortable in my clothes.

I hate what I see in the mirror.

I just want to like my body.

I'm the only one in my family that struggles with my weight.

No matter what I do, I don't look the way I want to.

Some of these admissions have stayed with me for a long time after I've had the conversations. They follow me around and pop into my head when I'm thinking of how I can better serve my clients. They bother me so much because I understand how scary they are to say out loud to another person, because at one point or another in my life, I've said many of the same things.

The hard truth is, you are never going to achieve the perfect body, because it doesn't exist in the real world. You might never have a perfectly flat stomach. Or arms that look lean and toned in a tank top. Your butt may always have dimples of cellulite and your thighs might brush up against each other. Your muffin top might always peek out above your jeans' waist band. And you will more than likely always have that awkward pinch of fat between your boobs and your armpits, because that is the bane of every single woman in the universe.

We pick at these things, grab at these things, and poke at them, hoping that if we acknowledge them enough, maybe spend enough hours obsessing over them, that they'll go away.

I'm not saying that to make you feel alone in your struggle, or to belittle your feelings of doubt about the way you look. I don't take these feelings lightly at all. They are very real, they are very frustrating, and they are also totally unproductive in helping you reach your full potential as the truly wonderful and beautiful human being that you are inside and out.

Your body is yours. It has imperfections, and flaws, but it would be so boring if we were all perfect! Women are brought up to think that there is always something wrong with us. The media picks apart female celebrities, and our culture encourages this. Read any popular feed's comments on Instagram, and you'll find people talking all kinds of crap about what's wrong with the female body in the photo. People are nasty. You know this. I know this. And we also know that when someone writes something nasty about another person's body, that it is only a reflection of how shitty they feel about their own looks. I can say this with assurance, because the minute I started liking the way I looked, I stopped picking other women apart inside my head and out loud through my speech.

Something you can do to encourage a shift in these feelings is to avoid negative people, and negative comments. Don't hang out with people who cut others down. Don't do it yourself. Anger and negativity just breed more of themselves when we let them come out. You don't have to love everything and everyone, but follow the saying "If you don't have anything nice to say, don't say anything at all." Put a sincere and positive spin on your comments towards others. Try to help others out when you can by focusing on what's great about them. They could probably use the help just as much as you! This habit will also make you more beautiful. Recognizing positive things about others helps you to grow your inner beauty, and you'll find you attract others who think the same way you do, which will only increase how great you feel about yourself.

You may also be in the very fortunate position of having loads of gorgeous friends, and chances are, if you think your friends are beautiful, they probably hold you in the same regard. I realize that maybe not all my friends are gorgeous by other people's standards, and for all I know we could just be a scraggly bunch of trolls, but the cool thing is that I look at the women in my life and truthfully think they *shine*.

If you look at the people you surround yourself with and see beauty in them, in their compassion, their actions and treatment of themselves and others, in the way they live their life, then you are very lucky. It's one more step on the road towards reaching your full potential because you appreciate that capacity in others.

If you consider the people in your life and instead feel disappointment, it's time to do the hard work of considering why that is. Are you hanging out with people who feel bad about themselves or make you feel negatively about yourself? Are you wasting time with people who have no ambition or desire to live a fulfilled life? These are not the traits of gorgeous friends, and you deserve to hang out with people you admire!

Once, while I was sitting in a group meditation, I began to have thoughts of resentment towards all my friends. Everyone seemed to be prettier than me, have more money, better relationships and jobs, an easier time achieving all the things I wanted for my own life. All of a sudden, I had a revelation; to my horror, I imagined what it would be like if none of my friends were successful or had good things happening to them, and how devastating that would be for me as well.

In a beautiful moment of clarity, I realized that all my jealous feelings could instead be shifted to a sense of pride in how great my friends were. In place of envying the things others close to me had achieved that I had not, I filled my heart up with pride that these incredible women would spend their time with me. I took ownership of how they made me want to push harder, and I knew they would be supportive of me when I realized my own triumphs.

It was one of the coolest moments of my life, sitting in silence amongst strangers, and letting all my bitterness flow out of me, to be replaced with renewed appreciation for the lovely people in my life. At the end of the meditation session, I floated back to the surface of reality feeling radiant.

I hope you think your friends are beautiful, and that they make you feel the same way. We all deserve to have strong and encouraging relationships with others. You are so beautiful. I know you are, without ever having met you, because you want something better and greater for yourself. I know you are beautiful, and you only have to see that for yourself to give truth to my words.

Realize how fantastic you are, with all your awesome imperfections and talents and cool flaws and assets, and transform your life, starting with how you see yourself.

How incredibly gorgeous are these women? I have had the great pleasure of working with every one of these ladies at one time or another, and they have so much beauty just radiating out of them. They are athletic, positive, and loving people, and not only do they light up every room they come into, but they have given me so much love and support along the way. I'm so lucky!

Interlude
You Have Nothing to
Worry About

IN MY LATE 20s, just three months into pole dancing, my studio director encouraged me sign up for a pole dancing competition. I signed up, not having any clue what I was getting myself into, put together a routine that included the only two pole tricks I knew at the time, and bedazzled an old t-shirt as my costume. One large misconception about pole dancing is that we wear little clothing in order to be "sexy" or whatever, but it's actually because the more skin that is exposed, the safer it is for the dancers. Skin grips on to the pole, so more skin equals more grip. The more you cover up, the bigger risk you run of slipping on the pole, missing a trick, and hurting yourself.

I grew up on stage, but not once in three decades, did I ever show even a hint of my stomach on stage. When I was young, if one of the girls at my dance school dared to bare her less than perfect midriff during a show, there would always be somebody whispering about her "rolls" backstage. I grew up among people who did not take their shirts off unless they had at least two abs showing.

The night of our dress rehearsal, we invited friends and family to come watch us. I hadn't performed on a stage by myself in fifteen years, and never in so little clothing. In an effort to conceal my most imperfect body part, my stomach, I had fashioned a piece of fabric to go across it diagonally in a way that I thought appeared artistic, but it kept getting tangled up or caught or twisted or making me slip on the pole, and a fellow dancer saw me struggling with it backstage.

"Why are you wearing this?" she asked.

"Because I don't want people to see my stomach," I replied sadly. "My friends and clients are out there. If they see my cellulite, they might make fun of me."

This moment, for all its sadness and beauty, is one of my favorite life moments. This friend, who is a beautiful thing of a human, grabbed me by both shoulders and looked me in the eye.

"You are beautiful, and you are strong, and you have nothing to worry about." she said to me.

And, wonderfully, I believed her.

I went on stage a few minutes later, with my sparkles and sports bra and short shorts, after quickly removing the troublesome piece of fabric, and I forgot to worry about what my stomach looked like or what people were thinking about me. For a few minutes, I danced my heart out, with all my flaws and all my imperfections on display, and I felt wonderful.

After the show, I was overwhelmed by how many people approached me. Friends told me they wished they could do that. Strangers told me they loved my performance. Clients commented on how strong I was. Not one person told me I should hide my stomach.

I learned some great lessons that night. I learned that the small act of telling another woman how beautiful she is has great power. In the short game, but in the long game, too. I learned that owning who you are will always be more beautiful than losing five more pounds. I learned that standing up in front of an audience and declaring what you have will empower others to do the same.

May you tell another woman she is beautiful. May she say it back to you.

2014: Once I stopped worrying about my tummy, I was able to have the best friggin' time on stage ever. This was my Top Gun routine, and I remember having a BLAST.
(Photography Credit: Alloy Images)

"Once we begin to celebrate what our body does rather than obsessing on how it looks, we start to appreciate our body as an instrument rather than an ornament."

—Ashley Turner

Chapter Five
Capabilities and Imperfections

Part One: Body Capable

Stop thinking about what your body looks like and start considering what it CAN DO.

You heard me! More often than I'd like, women who I think are amazing, talented, athletic, strong, inspiring humans, will lament their physical appearance. "But you can do this, and this, and THIS!" I'll cry! Too often we forget to be thankful for the gift of movement, which not everyone has. We focus on those five extra pounds, that little roll of fat under our butts, the way our arms jiggle a little when we wave. We so easily see these teeny tiny things that are considered wrong, and it blinds us to all that is awesome about us. Just like that junior-high boy telling me I was plain got into my head for years, we repeat belittling things to ourselves that create very real deficits in our confidence.

I read somewhere once, "There is nothing more boring than people talking about how fat they are." I remember it because it's so true. Seriously, I don't want to hear about how you are not completely perfect! I want to hear about the new fitness class you were scared of but tried anyways! I want to hear about how you took yourself on a trip to Thailand! I want to hear about how you taught your kid the difference between right and wrong last night! I want to hear about how you had great luck finding parking today!

Anything you could tell me about your life would be more interesting than having to listen to you tell me how not-awesome you are, because I know different. You are seriously awesome, my dear reader, in so many ways. I am so inspired by your courage, your zeal, your fire, your capabilities! I am thrilled you are reading this!

If I'm being impartial to my theory though, I admit that to a certain degree, looks matter. Let's not pretend they don't.

There! I said it! But before you throw this little book away and denounce me as a huge fraud, hang on just a second.

Looks matter, but they aren't the only thing that counts. Seriously. Whatever you look like stops mattering the minute you show me how lovely you are inside. That's how I think of peoples' beauty all the time. And that is also what matters to the kind of people you want in your life, if you let them see that beauty. Forget about the people who can't see past your looks. They are not your tribe. They won't have your back no matter what you look like, because that judgement they're passing is all about them and not at all about you. And the second you take it back, and belittle yourself to nothing more than a number on the scale, is the same second that you need to remind yourself of what you're capable of.

Are you capable of:

Moving? Walking? Squatting? Carrying your child? Hugging? Walking with your prosthetic leg? Doing a cartwheel? Dancing? Running? Helping a friend move? Carrying groceries upstairs? Stretching? Lifting weights in your wheelchair? Holding your spouse's handbags? Clapping? Climbing? Downward Dog? Writing? Pole dancing? Completing a 5K? Crossing the street with your crutches? Throwing a Frisbee? Dancing at a wedding? Completing your physical therapy? Smiling?

Because if you answered "Yes" to even some of these, then you my friend, have an amazing body, and *you* are body capable!

It does the things it's supposed to. And probably more. It surprises you all the time with what it can make it through and what it's capable of. Give your body a little appreciation and a whole lot of credit for all the things it can do.

I have recently adopted a morning ritual that can also help you to exercise your body-appreciation muscle. On my commute to work, I try and think of three things that I'm grateful for. These three things don't have to be different or new every time, but it helps me to remember what I have going for me. I encourage you to begin this practice, and remind yourself of all the things you are grateful for, including what your body is capable of. They can range from small to big; perhaps you are grateful that you can walk pain free to work, that you were able to climb the stairs to your office with strength in your legs, that you signed up for a yoga class on your lunch hour, that you kept up with your dog on a recent beach run, or that you hit a personal best in the gym over the weekend. The only limit to the cool things your body is capable of is how much you appreciate it, recognize it, and honor it.

Remember that we are focusing our goals on achievements that have nothing to do with looks. As long as you're making healthy choices, what matters more than your pant size is what your body is capable of doing when you ask it to do something. That's how I think of people's beauty all the time. And that's how others will think of you, if you let them.

Several years ago when I first became certified as a personal trainer, I told a friend that my goal was to get a "good enough body" to be able to run my upcoming half marathon with just a sports bra as a top. I was determined to lose enough weight so that my stomach wouldn't be a source of embarrassment and a distraction from enjoying the event, and I had somehow convinced myself that being able to show your midsection to others was a privilege only reserved for those with six pack abs. I felt so bad about myself the day of the race, when I hadn't managed to achieve the look I was going for and ended up covering myself up with a tank top. Looking back, this is so laughable and disappointing to me. Instead of reminding myself how lucky I was to have a body that was strong enough to run 13.1 miles, I was worried what strangers might think if I trotted past them with a little cellulite on my tummy. It seems ironic and yet so fitting to me that down the road I chose to participate in a sport like pole dancing, where the safety of the athletes is often determined by how much skin is exposed, and that I ended up spending the last few years prancing around on stage in the equivalent of my underwear. It's so silly to me that at one point in my life I chose to hide a part of myself that I felt ashamed of instead of enjoying the activity I was engaged in while being in comfortable clothing.

Oftentimes, it is only when we lose an ability that we appreciate what we had. Reflect for a moment on instances that have or could have altered how you feel physically. Think back to when you have been ill or injured. Perhaps having children or an operation or growing older affected your energy levels or changed your body. Time and financial constraints can impact our opportunities for body capabilities. So can learning disabilities, natural coordination, or occurrences that caused us fear and shifted what we were physically able to handle. Our body capabilities can change in an instant, so let's appreciate and focus on what we can do at present, instead of our trivial physical flaws.

Part Two: You Are Awesomely Imperfect

If denying yourself a glass of wine every night sounds like the most awful thing in the world, don't do it. If you feel sick after eating a half (or a whole) pizza, don't do that that either. Listen to your body, and to your emotions that go along with your actions. Let those be your guides when it comes to making healthy choices for yourself, and you'll start to feel better about what's looking back at you in the mirror.

My imperfections are what make me who I am. My goofy toothy smile. My tummy fluff. My muscular legs that will always scream weightlifter and never ballerina. These are the things that make me who I am. I cannot change them. And you cannot change who you are in the depths of your core, because these little flaws and story tellers are a part of you.

I am not perfect. You are not perfect. No one is perfect. Phew! Isn't that a relief!? The minute you truly make peace with that belief will be the minute your life changes forever and for better. People probably tell you that all the time, but believing and accepting it is really an accomplishment. Everybody looks different, and every person has different thoughts and feelings and challenges that they deal with daily.

Your imperfections, both mentally and physically, are what make you uniquely you. They are what make you human, and more compassionate and understanding towards others.

Your mind and body tell a story. Your scars, your cellulite, the shape of your butt, they all say something about who you are, what choices you make, and how you feel about yourself. You can either choose to remember the moments that have made you who you are, or you can start to change your story.

It's time to stop hating your body for all that it "isn't" and time to start being grateful for all that it does. Stop beating yourself up and picking on everything that's "wrong" with you. Instead of hating on the only thing we're guaranteed to have for the rest of our lives, why don't we take pause, and say thank you to that hardworking machine for all that it does for us.

I want you to make peace with your body, whatever stage you are at in life. It's so easy to compare ourselves to our skinniest, our fittest, our youngest prettiest self, but in order to appreciate your looks, and who you are, it's important to make peace with the body you currently have. Your body is not all bad or all good, it's just human. The next time you're about to hate on your body, or anything about your looks, or turn down a compliment, instead, remind yourself of one awesome thing that your body did for you lately. Our bodies don't ask a lot of us, and in return, they allow us to do some amazing things. It's a funny thing, but the more love and gratitude you show your body, the more beautiful you'll end up being.

"It was in the air, or so it seemed to Kiki, this hatred of women and their bodies- it seeped in with every draught in the house; people brought it home on their shoes, they breathed it in off their newspapers. There was no way to control it."

—Zadie Smith, *On Beauty*

Interlude
You Must Have a Wide Ribcage

AT FOURTEEN, I was in a pre-professional ballet company. This wasn't your average hometown dance recital crew, let me tell you. Most of the young women and men I danced with went on to become principal dancers in the greatest ballet companies in the world. But not me. I didn't have the right body type to be a ballerina.

I was good, too. But I had boobs, and no matter what I did, I couldn't seem to get my curvy body to look like the other girls'. We would all gather around to look at the pictures from our recitals, and my heart would always fall in disappointment. In one picture, in particular, all the girls were in matching white tutus and had their backs to the camera. We all had the exact same costume, pose, hairstyle, form, everything. One girl pointed at the largest girl in the picture.

"You can tell that's Natalie!" she said, laughing, "because she has such a wide ribcage!"

Ribcage. Boobs. Fat. Whatever it was, it all added up to me not looking like the other girls, and not getting the parts that I wanted. My ballet directors had been making similar comments for months, and I'm sure she'd overheard them say something like that and had just repeated it.

One way or another, I started to get the impression that if I lost weight, I would get better roles. With my agreement, my mom and I started the Atkins diet that was popular in the 90s. Nowadays, the Atkins Diet has evolved a lot and is not unreasonable, but at that time, before we knew more about health, we put ourselves on a highly restrictive diet which felt like it consisted of steak, heavy whipping cream, eggs, and something ridiculous like one slice of cucumber a day.

The diet book said I would go through something called "ketosis." Basically, this means I would eat so much steak and heavy whipping cream that my body would perform some type of magic that would make me feel like crap but I would look incredible. That is not at all a scientific explanation but I feel my summarization of this subject is more fun.

So I went through ketosis, and not only was I exhausted, but I was super constipated. I dropped fifteen pounds in a month on this diet but didn't take a shit the entire time. I kept thinking that if only I could go to the bathroom, I probably would have doubled that weight loss number.

And the whole month I was on this horrible eating plan, my ballet directors were just cooing over how wonderful I looked, literally poking at my body where there used to be more fat and saying how great I looked and how I was finally living up to my potential.

But a gal can only take so much. After four weeks of not pooping, I hopped in the car with my dad one afternoon and insisted he take me to Starbucks for a Cranberry Bliss Bar. To this day, Cranberry Bliss Bars are still the greatest thing I eat all year long. They taste like sugary-carb-loaded freedom.

I put every pound I had lost back on in two weeks. My ballet directors returned to scowling at me. I returned to regular bathroom visits and carbohydrates and fiber.

I look back on that month and marvel at how long I stuck it out before realizing that no amount of discomfort was worth obtaining a look that my body wasn't ready for. It makes me realize how much other women put themselves through, just trying to achieve a certain figure and please others, because I have been there. There is a difference between eating healthy and torturing yourself. It's okay to go after your goal, and to make sacrifices to achieve it, as long as they are sacrifices you are willing to make, and that goal is something that makes your life better in a very real way.

1999: My friend helped me hook up the corset of my costume to make sure my "wide ribcage" didn't bust out of my dress. Let's also take a moment and notice that I had already developed size D cups, which made me feel even more out of place and overweight in comparison with the other girls I danced with.

"A consequence of female self-love is that the woman grows convinced of social worth. Her love for her body will be unqualified, which is the basis of female identification. If a woman loves her own body, she doesn't grudge what other women do with theirs; if she loves femaleness, she champions its rights. It's true what they say about women: Women *are* insatiable.

We *are* greedy. Our appetites do need to be controlled if things are to stay in place. If the world were ours too, if we believed we could get away with it, we *would* ask for more love, more sex, more money, more commitment to children, more food, more care.

These sexual, emotional, and physical demands *would* begin to extend to social demands: payment for care of the elderly, parental leave, childcare, etc.

The force of female desire would be so great that society would truly have to reckon with what women want, in bed and in the world." —Naomi Wolf, *The Beauty Myth*

Chapter Six
Classifying Behaviors

A BIG FACTOR in how women feel about themselves is the act of separating their behavior into categories. I'm unsure of when I began this habit myself, but through conversations with other women, I know it is a commonality for many of us. Classifying behaviors means mentally separating our behaviors into divisions of what is acceptable in order to maintain or change our appearance.

We tend to classify behaviors into good and bad. Examples of "good" behaviors are things like exercising, drinking plenty of water, eating vegetables, avoiding carbs. Examples of "bad" behaviors are reaching into the bread basket at a restaurant, drinking alcohol during the week, missing spin class to watch television, driving instead of walking. Many of us were taught this behavior as children, that junk food was "a treat," or we weren't allowed to have sugar in the house because it was "a temptation," or the classic "no dessert unless you finish your dinner." We are taught that these behaviors fall into two classifications of succeeding or failing, and then we lose either way.

What is true of many people, is that they will go through a period of eating healthy, exercising a lot, and feeling great about themselves. Then all of a sudden, they will eat some unhealthy food, or miss a workout, and it feels as if they've undone all their hard work. Instead of moving on from one treat, they'll give up and eat junk the rest of the day or even the week. While they could have made up their work out later, they'll start finding excuses to miss more and more exercise. Because it is entrenched in our brain that we must be all good or all bad to succeed or fail, one misstep and most people give up.

So many women I've spoken with suffer from this collapse in willpower that makes them feel terrible about themselves. Eating a bowl of ice cream or some French fries or missing a workout translates into "well, I might as well give up now," and so we struggle regaining our ability to feel empowered and in control. Instead of recognizing the reality of the situation, that a few hundred calories will not actually have a marked effect on our bodies, our health, or how we fit into our jeans, we judge ourselves based on the messages we've been told. It's about that sense of failing to be perfect, to follow the rules of whatever game we've been taught to play to win the prize of the world thinking we met its standards. It isn't a game any of us can win, and yet so many of us, myself included at times, have played it.

I'm reminded of the classic Amy Schumer "I'm So Bad" comedy sketch, where four women sit around a restaurant table and lament what food choices they've made recently while the rest of them reassure their friends that they look great. It starts out normally enough, with one woman verbally regretting how many fries she ate at their meal and declaring "I'm so bad!" It deteriorates quickly in a spiral of increasingly worse food choices accompanied by even worse moral choices, with the women stating the junk food they've eaten to go along with things like cyber bullying teenagers and watching strangers commit suicide. Finally, an unsuspecting waiter approaches the table to offer dessert to the ladies, and they proceed to cannibalize him while berating themselves for how bad they're being.

How many of us have done this with ourselves and our friends? No, not the cannibalism part. I'm sure there's a book for that. The part where we worry more about whether what we eat makes us a bad person, or worse, whether we value our food choices and appearance more than our actions and thoughts. Instead of pondering if we acted in accordance with our morals and with treating others with compassion, we judge our worth based on what we ate and how it affected what we look like. In her incredibly eloquent and thoughtful article, "Food Choices Aren't Moral Issues—Here's How to Stop Making Kids Think They Are" by Ellen Friedrichs, the author points out several problems with the language we currently use to discuss food and how it relates to people's value.

"...while we may have beliefs about how we would like to eat, not following these a hundred percent of the

time, or not adhering to them at every turn, doesn't mean we have failed.

"We're all accustomed to ads for products we are told are 'sinfully' delicious or a 'guilty' pleasure. And everyone has at least a passing familiarity with the claims that everything from juices to granola bars are 'pure,' 'natural,' or even 'cleansing'.

"Now, picking the cookie over the kale is not just a matter of taste and nutrition. It is also an issue of willpower and strength of character. Choosing the budget yogurt over the organic isn't only about finances, but also about virtue."

Right on the money, sister. I could not have said it better myself. It's okay to believe that you should eat certain foods and avoid other ones. It's okay to strive to exercise and move on a regular basis even when it's often more convenient to stay immobile. But skipping a beat on these actions shouldn't make us feel worth less.

It is healthier to enjoy all things in moderation, and not indulge too much or get too immobile due to a single slip up. These are two keys to feeling better about ourselves over all. I think if we focus on choosing what makes our lives and ourselves better in the long run, versus categorizing actions as either all good or all bad, it will be easier to bounce back to live a healthy-all-things-in-moderation life.

I know this is harder to do than it is to say and advise. We all have different things that are tough for us to do and to keep doing, and the feeling that if we don't do these things that we won't look the way we want is very strong. My advice for you is to make the best decisions you can and make those decisions for yourself and nobody else. Find a pattern that works for you and trust in it. Whatever you decide is the right answer.

I believe the first step in changing the classification of behaviors starts with acknowledgement. I admittedly do this, whether it's because I'm trying to mimic the language that my clients and friends use, or because I feel it myself. Instead of telling yourself or friends how "bad" you're being by getting fries on the side instead of the garden salad, stop that thought in its tracks. As opposed to forcing yourself to exercise or risking feeling guilty about not going to the gym, attempt to incorporate movement as a regular staple in your life in ways that feel natural. Rather than feeling bad about yourself, feel entitled to question both your decision and your feelings surrounding it. You can ask yourself questions such as:

- ➢ How does eating this food/working out make me feel?

- ➢ Am I making this choice for myself or others?

- ➢ How will I feel after I make this choice?

- ➢ Will I punish/reward myself for this choice, or simply continue to live out my day?

- ➢ Is there a better choice I could make for myself right now, or is this choice, while perhaps not ideal, the best and most appropriate one for me to make in this moment?

It may sound silly to consider these questions when all we are talking about here is eating and exercising. But for many of us, it isn't as simple as eating and exercising. We are measuring our self-worth by the standards of what we feed ourselves, how many hours we spend at the gym, and how our actions measure up to the standards of a perfect body. These issues have become complicated, so let's grant ourselves permission to acknowledge that the tendency to entangle our behaviors with our value is real, and address it.

A lot of fitness professionals are trying to change the way we think about these actions in an effort not to demonize behaviors that make people feel like they've messed up. It's very difficult though. The fitness industry is often associated with fast results, strict programs, and perfection. Every time a female client comes to me looking beautiful and simultaneously expressing how losing some weight would make her feel better, I struggle with how to approach the topic. For so many years when I was confronted with this common request to "just lose a few pounds," I would do my best to provide quality workouts to these women and leave it at that.

Nowadays, when I'm told this common fitness goal, I deliberately pause and remind that client how valuable and beautiful they are. I can usually find something I genuinely admire in most people I meet, so I don't use these words superficially. But it can't just end there. The question of how to make these women feel beautiful inside and out needs to be a conversation that we have in the fitness industry, and other fields as well. People often think they seek out fitness professionals to make a physical change, and often that's true, but many times it's because deep down they just want to feel better about themselves. When clients come to us using language like "muffin tops," "belly rolls," "flabby arms," "thigh gap," and "bikini bridge," it's usually so engrained in their way of thinking that the process of getting rid of those terms is more of a challenge than getting through the workouts. A good fitness professional doesn't just see what areas of your body you want to improve, they spot the reasons WHY you want to improve them. I also believe that it is our duty in my industry to provide help on both fronts, and it took me a long time to realize that only focusing on one or the other was doing a disservice to both ourselves as the example setters and leaders, and to the people who come to us seeking help.

If you're ready to choose a different internal dialogue to have with yourself about food, then I commend you. I am with you on this journey. Continue to press forward on this road to valuing yourself based on who you are and your actions, rather than what you ate or if you did all your workouts this week. Balance is beautiful, whatever that means to you. If you want to help change the dialogue we use when talking about food and our bodies, join the conversation at www.barbellblondie.com.

Interlude
Are You Looking For A Personal Trainer?

I LIKED RUNNING on the treadmill.

During my first job after college, I would wake up at 5:00 a.m., drive to my local gym, and run exactly three miles on the treadmill before heading home to get ready for work. I loved it. I loved counting down the mileage and trying to sprint my way to the finish. I felt so great all day, so energized. My pants fit well, I had moved into my very first apartment on my own, and I was feeling good about things.

One morning I checked into the gym, and an employee stopped me at the front desk.

"Are you looking for a personal trainer?" he asked. I smiled timidly, nervous because this cute guy was talking to me, and shook my head no as I accepted the business card he handed to me. "Because I see you in here every morning, working hard," he continued, "and it doesn't look like you're getting the results you want."

EVERY. BODY. BEAUTIFUL.

My face fell. The sun wasn't even up yet, and this random man whom I'd never seen in my life was telling me I wasn't good enough. I wasn't sure what I wasn't good enough at, but I was aware that I was being insulted, and that I was a victim of a poor attempt at a sales pitch.

Ironically, at the time I don't think I even understood what a personal trainer was, I just knew that I enjoyed running, and didn't really have a goal or plan in place. I just wanted to run, that was all. His comment made me feel stupid, like he'd just let me in on the fact that I still wasn't measuring up to the world's standard of beauty. Surprise! You're still just plain and now a little bit chubby, too. It was that boy in eighth grade telling me I wasn't good enough all over again.

"Don't insult someone if you want their business" I shot back at him, and walked over to the trashcan to throw his business card in. Running made me feel great about myself, and I wouldn't let this person take that away from me. And yes! I really was that sassy to him. Sassiness is a trait we should all unleash from time to time.

2011: Crossing the finish line of my favorite half marathon in Anaheim. Running puts a smile on my face! This is how movement and physical accomplishments should make us feel.

"Whatever is deeply, essentially female-the life in a woman's expression, the feel of her flesh, the shape of her breasts, the transformations after childbirth of her skin-is being reclassified as ugly, and ugliness as disease. These qualities are about an intensification of female power, which explains why they are being recast as a diminution of power.

At least a third of a woman's life is marked with aging; about a third of her body is made of fat. Both symbols are being transformed into operable condition--*so that* women will only feel healthy if we are two thirds of the women we could be."

—Naomi Wolf, *The Beauty Myth*

Chapter Seven
Don't Be Ashamed of
Your Goals

I ONCE RECEIVED an email off my website from a gal who was looking for help to gain strength. Her email said she was embarrassed to talk about her goals specifically in writing, and asked if I could please call her.

When I got on the phone with her, she admitted to me that she had trouble keeping weight on, and that she was often mocked for her slender proportions by others.

"I realize this is a problem a lot of women are envious of," she told me, "but when I try to ask advice on how to put on muscle and gain weight to look healthier, people just end up making me feel ashamed, like I should be grateful that I'm not constantly trying to lose weight. I want to look the way I want to look too, but I feel bad about wanting this."

EVERY. BODY. BEAUTIFUL.

Wow, I thought to myself, *what a beautiful human!* I couldn't wait to meet her. I assured her that yes, her problem was considered a blessing by many women, but that if she wanted to become stronger and gain weight in a healthy way, that she should never let anyone make her feel embarrassed about that.

I am happy to tell you that she was able to gain muscle and become stronger, and feel more confident about herself on a daily basis, as well as in the gym. She stopped worrying about people accusing her of not eating. She was as beautiful inside and out as I thought she would be.

I share this story with you, because while there is plenty of body shaming that has occurred for decades in our culture of telling women they need to look a certain way or else they are not attractive, I believe there is an equal amount of shaming directed at women who are trying to change their bodies in one way or another.

This shaming goes after a large spectrum of fitness goals, with a wide range of who we target. New moms are body shamed when they're told to get their pre-baby bodies back. Then, when post-natal women announce that they are working towards conditioning their body or show their progress pictures to others, they are immediately told, "No! Don't change! Don't feel bad about what you look like! You're a mom now. Your priorities should be different than how you feel about your looks!" They can't win.

Another example is women on the petite side who want to make changes. I put myself in this category.

While I have never been what the medical field defines as "overweight," I have always struggled between my desire to eat all the things and enjoy wine, and still maintain my athletic physique. A couple of pounds makes a large difference on small women.

Anytime I start pushing myself to cut body fat for whatever reason, my goal is met with cries of, "You're so small already! Don't you ever give yourself a break?!" When I'm "fluffy" or carrying a few extra pounds around my midsection (my weight fluctuates on a ten-pound range throughout the year, depending on competition season and events), people glance disapprovingly at my midsection when I tell them I'm a personal trainer. There are always some people I can't win with either way. Either society is telling me I'm working too hard and look good enough already, or they're disapproving of me not working hard enough. There is no middle ground.

These are just a few examples of body shaming that I see all the time. If someone wants to change the way they look because it makes them feel better, and they're doing it in a healthy way, than what do the rest of us care if they want to make that change? Seriously, it in no way affects anyone else. So let's stop the body shaming and telling women that they need to look one way or another, but let's also stop telling women to deny themselves goals of looking a certain way, whether or not we think they look good. It's not up to us. We are all on our own journeys.

Now, if you honestly think another woman is beautiful just the way she is, by all means share that with her! I love telling my friends how gorgeous I think they are, whether they are sharing a goal with me or not. I only wish that more of them believed me when I told them.

One of my favorite things to do is to give people compliments. I will compliment someone on the bus on her shoes, a waitress on her hair, a friend on her laugh. Compliment others on things you like about them, and when on the receiving end of a compliment, accept it. Hand in hand with this, if someone shares with you something that they are proud of, don't just say congratulations and move on. Recognize that this is something they are proud of, and try to ask some follow up questions to celebrate how awesome their achievement is. This is another way of complimenting someone, to sincerely recognize what they think is great about themselves and paying attention to it.

I think it's pretty common to go through a whole day without having one single person say something nice to you, and so just in case they don't realize how awesome they are, I like to remind people. Sometimes I will be having a difficult moment, and all it takes is a kind stranger saying something nice to me that reminds me how good I have it. We all need that boost from time to time. Perhaps if more people paid each other compliments, we would all feel a little less self-doubt, feel a little more confident, and a lot more beautiful.

It definitely takes some guts to compliment a stranger, but I promise you, they are not going to yell at you to leave them alone or say how much they hate being told nice things about themselves. I have yet to compliment a stranger and have them do anything besides burst into a smile and thank me. Sometimes that's all we have to say to each other. Sometimes it begins a great random conversation. Sometimes they'll pay it forward with another small act of kindness. Sometimes that person reappears later on my life in the most strange and coincidental way, and the only reason we remember one another is because I reached out to them in an elevator one time to pay them a compliment.

Please accept compliments that come your way. Now let me be clear, I am not talking about catcalls or harassment on the street. I am not talking about letting someone belittle you and turn you into a sex object without your consent. I am speaking solely about someone who intends you nothing but kindness and well wishes. You know the difference. It always makes me a little sad when I extend a compliment and that person refuses to accept it, and instead cuts themselves down. When I tell a friend she's beautiful, and she disagrees, it makes me sad, and it also makes me not want to give her any more compliments. A compliment is a gift that costs nothing. You rejecting a compliment is your way of telling that person that you think less of yourself than they do. It tells the world you don't value yourself to believe what they had to say.

Next time someone tells you something nice about yourself, even if you don't feel you deserve it, just say "thank you" and smile. You deserve it.

EVERY. BODY. BEAUTIFUL.

At Pole Sport Organization's 2016 National Competition, my dream was to dress up as a cat with a huge sparkly rainbow tail. I knew it wouldn't win the competition, but it was the goal I knew would make me happiest
I've never had so much fun on stage, and I very gratefully accepted the bronze medal that night. If you want to be a sparkly rainbow kitty, then go after it! Don't let anyone tell you what your goals can or can't be!

"Create the highest, grandest vision possible for your life, because you become what you believe."

—Oprah Winfrey

Chapter Eight
Create Positivity in Your Life

YOU ARE THE ONLY person standing between you and your happiness, self-worth, and beauty. Whether you are a drama queen, or just feeling a little lost, whether you have some serious shit going on in your life, or need to seek professional help to get you through whatever you're going through, the solution is always you.

I have wrestled with all of these things. I have gone through some truly dark moments, but in truth, I have also created many of my own problems. All those years I spent thinking I was plain and average were a waste of time I could have spent feeling better. It's too late to dwell on the past, but it's the perfect time to create some serious shifts in your life now, for the present and a future where you can appreciate yourself. What makes us good people, is when we recognize that there are better choices for us to make and we go out and make them!

If you are not waking up every single day with so much gratitude about the blessings of your life, then I am telling you, it's time to make some changes. You've got to look in the mirror and be able to think you are the luckiest, most wonderful person. I'm not saying you are an ungrateful person. Not at all. For many years, I was unable to see the pure beauty and adventure that was my life because I was looking through the clouded dark lenses of my untreated anxiety and depression. This didn't make me a bad person or ungrateful. It just meant I had to figure out my own unique and personal obstacles to find out how to see clearly.

Ask yourself some questions:

➢ Have I asked for help?

➢ Can you reflect on your day and feel like you were your best self?

➢ Are you doing one thing you love every day?

➢ Do you wake up excited and inspired by your job?

➢ Are you consistently learning new things and hearing new ideas?

➢ Do you feel like the people you surround yourself with excite you or bring you down?

Have I asked for help?

As I said, some of you reading this will be in the midst of serious problems, and you may feel hopeless about what your options are. If you feel like this, I encourage you to ask for help, from anyone and everyone that you trust. It's possible that you're not sure what is wrong, but you know you're miserable.

No matter the case, it is okay to ask for help.

Reach out to family, friends, colleagues, or you can even post something on Facebook these days if you're comfortable with that. You can send an email, a letter, a text, a phone call, anything. Too often we think that if we ask for help that this is a sign of weakness, but I believe it shows genuine strength to admit you are imperfect and would like to allow others to assist you. You may have been trying to solve a problem only looking at it from certain angles. Let someone you trust take a peek and see what they find.

Can you reflect on your day and feel like you were your best self?

You won't always be your best self. Not every day will be the best day ever. You will make mistakes every single day. But every night I go to sleep knowing that I'm going to be better and stronger the next morning, and that I will learn from my mistakes. Sometimes I figure it out right away, and sometimes it takes me longer. But I am always trying to be my best self.

So start to think about your day. Did you make a healthy choice instead of one that made you feel bad mentally and physically? Did you help others when you had an opportunity to do so? Were you kind when it would have been easy to be rude? Did you treat others with respect, but stick up for yourself when you knew you deserved it also? Most importantly, did you respect and love yourself? Did you invest in your self-worth by being your own biggest cheerleader?

Try to live your days being proud of how you got through them. We are never perfect, but we are faced with hundreds of choices every day, and it's up to us to make the best ones we can. If you are going to bed at night, feeling ashamed of something you did, of how you treated yourself or another human, try to make amends if possible, especially if it includes forgiving yourself.

Are you doing one thing you love every single day?

You are? Awesome! Gold Star for you! You aren't?! For heaven's sake why not?

Life is full of crappy, adult-ish responsibilities that take up time and energy and drain us. It's important to invest in yourself for at least a small amount of time every single day, so that you can be your best self.

How does doing one thing you love every single day help you to have positive body image and feel beautiful? Imagine yourself as you are right now. Picture yourself in your mind, including all your imperfections, and all the things you wish were different, especially on your worst days.

Now, imagine yourself doing an activity that you love and enjoy. This activity can be anything. It can be movement, relaxing at the beach, drinking a glass of wine, spending time with loved ones, reading a book, walking outside, playing with a pet, shopping, getting a massage, anything at all. As long as this thing you imagine brings you joy, you should do it. Now that imaginary you is enjoying an activity, think about how you feel. Do you feel lighter, more joyful, kinder? Do you feel more energetic, more loved, more capable, stronger?

Does this version of you feel more beautiful?

Now, if imaginary you benefitted from all these things, I bet real you would as well. When you take care of yourself, it relieves stress and brings you joy. When you are happier, that energy exudes out of you. You are more likely to stay relaxed, to be compassionate and kind towards others, and to be able to handle things that come your way. You are able to finish your day, look in the mirror at yourself, and be reminded that you were the best version of yourself you could be. You made the world around you better too, because happy people create better energy. All of this, because you took time to do something you loved during your day.

Do you wake up excited and inspired by your job?

Because you should! Now, I'm not saying that you will love every second of every work day. I'm not saying there will not be things you have to take care of that are annoying and frustrating and time consuming and boring. But if you are waking up every day, wishing you didn't have to go to work, hating your job, hating people you work with, then let's examine that.

Essentially, I want you to examine whether you aren't enjoying your job because it's not the right job for you, or if it's because you haven't given it a fair chance. Either way, begin to find ways that you can enjoy it more, either by becoming more a part of the team, asking permission to work on a special assignment that really revs you up, or speaking to your supervisor about possible other positions or learning opportunities. I really encourage you to spend your precious time working in a career you love. It's not just that you spend so much of your life at work, but working a job that you enjoy and thrive at will boost your confidence!

Are you consistently learning new things and hearing new ideas?

Something that makes people very unattractive to me, is when they are stale, set in their ways, and closed off to the opinions of others. You can put the most physically attractive person in the room with me, and the minute I figure out they think they know everything and aren't open to learning anything new, they suddenly gross me out. I stop associating with them, because I don't want their staleness to rub off on me.

I'm not talking about people who have different opinions than me. Different opinions are what make the world interesting! But when I meet someone who can not recognize that there is so much we can learn from one another, they offer me little value. This says that they aren't open to possibilities, which says they don't see their full potential and self-worth.

Be the other kind of person, and you'll soon discover how attractive you can be to many people.

Today, someone who is willing to try something different, admit they need to learn more, or listen and engage with other humans who think and feel differently from them is a very rare, and very beautiful thing. Listening to others and how they feel can simply be called kindness. When you are kind to others, you hold them in positive regard and wish them happiness.

Next time you're struggling with something, ask others what they think you may be able to learn to help you. Oftentimes the answers are all around us, and are quite accessible, if only we admit that we need someone to help us find those answers. They may recommend a book to read, a class to take, or a documentary to watch. Try following through and taking their advice, and then bring it up to them later. When I take someone's advice and let them know that I listened to what they had to say, it always enhances my relationship with them, and makes me feel stronger and more beautiful.

Ask these questions of yourself on a regular basis, and the answers may help you to be your best self. Many times we are the biggest obstacle in our own lives, and shifting our perspective on how we feel and think can influence how we feel about ourselves as well.

Do you feel like the people you surround yourself with excite you or bring you down?

If you are surrounded by people who can't wait to spend time with you, then congrats, because you have it made! Cherish those connections and tell those people how much you appreciate them because being someone that others want to be around is certainly special.

Many times in my life, I've been surrounded by people who wanted to bring me down, and I would always leave our interactions feeling worse than when I arrived. Friends who just wanted to gossip and complain. Co-workers who blamed everyone else for their lack of success and issues at the office. Boyfriends who left me constantly questioning my worth and their intentions. It shouldn't be like that. These people are energy vampires that drain strength and awesomeness out of the lives of others. They are not your tribe. At the time, I didn't realize that's who I was surrounding myself with. When I started to strive for more though, to make changes in my own life, it became glaringly obvious who was not going to come along for the ride. One of the best parts of being your best self and living that life is that you get to decide what you will accept and what you won't.

If the people around you are not having honest and genuine conversations with you that go deeper than pleasantries and catching up, if you worry about whether you can trust someone or not or if they have your best interests at heart, or if you've invited them to spend one-on-one time with you more than once and they've declined repeatedly, you are officially done with them. This doesn't make these people bad people. It just makes them people you don't want in your life right now. Begin to have expectations of who you want to have around, and you will find out if others will rise to the occasion. Maybe someone will surprise you, and your relationship will become deeper and more solidified. But if not, I promise you, there are literally millions of wonderful people out there that can't wait to know someone as incredible as yourself, and you'll never get to meet them if you keep hanging out with people who bring you down. Having quality people around you will reinforce your self-worth.

When your relationships are equal, you are going to feel great about yourself. Receiving love and positivity from others will reinforce what you are working towards, and giving that love back will make you so beautiful.

"Beauty is not in the face; beauty is a light in the heart."

—Kahlil Gibran

Conclusion
Every. Body. Beautiful.

I SEE YOU. You are not alone. You are not the only one who struggles to feel adequate and attractive enough. I see what you are up against and I recognize it and I encourage you to transform how you view yourself. We are up against a lifetime of images and messages that have told us we are not good enough. It is so ingrained in our language and our thoughts that a mental makeover won't happen overnight, but with effort and time, we can all strengthen our ability to love ourselves and appreciate the beautiful bodies we are blessed with. When you start to feel down about yourself, or you judge someone else, make every effort to replace those negative thoughts with something positive and compassionate. I guarantee this will improve your quality of life.

It's not that I want to encourage you to maybe, sort of, kind of, mull all of this information over and get around to feeling better about yourself one day. I am telling you, shouting at you, that you NEED TO REALIZE IMMEDIATELY how incredible you are. You have to realize it as soon as humanly possible, because the world needs you to see it, so that you can go out and live your life and share the gospel with other women who need to hear this message. We need more women to appreciate themselves, so that they can set a new standard of confidence and love for everyone else out there who is struggling. I will stand up and be the loud yelling lady who thinks this is big deal.

I mean it with all my heart when I say that beauty is a glow that builds up within you and shines out beyond you. Be brave, and put yourself out there as much as you can. Take ownership of your body, your looks, and who you truly are. Acknowledge what feels imperfect about you and then accept yourself. Continue fighting to recognize these qualities, and your life will change.

You are fully capable of being beautiful, but you also have to rise on your feet, stand up, and acknowledge that beauty within others. Find the beauty in those around you, in their actions and humanity. Encourage those around you to recognize their own worth. Taking action starts with us, but to expand it past ourselves is where change really starts to take effect. Please share this book with others who might benefit from its message. There is a whole world out there with many people who could use a little more positivity and self-love in their lives. It would be so amazing if you were the one to ignite that within others!

If you don't like the way you look, talk to people you love and trust to help give you some perspective. So many of us feel similarly, and together, we may be able to realize a different conviction. Reflect on the pieces of your story that make you feel one way or another about yourself and take ownership of those feelings. Visualize that everybody is beautiful. Put the actions from this book into motion and start to appreciate who you are. You are a part of something bigger, and the world needs you to love and value yourself. You are exceptional.

It all starts with you.

2017: Me, feeling beautiful.
(Photography Credit: Billy Polson)

Gratitude

COUNTLESS CONVERSATIONS went into creating this book.

Thank you to my mom for taking her time to edit my book not once but twice. She has been my editor since I first began writing as a kiddo, and I'm so glad she could help me with this project. She also put up with me during what I'm sure were some very frustrating teenage years when I didn't like myself very much, so she deserves a few extra thank yous for that as well. Thank you. Thank you. Thank you again.

Thank you to the community of women I call my friends and family. Every one of you pushes me to think harder, create more, and question what I know. You ladies are seriously the coolest most bad ass bitches ever.

References

Atkins, Robert C. (1981). *Dr. Atkins' Diet Revolution*. New York, NY: Bantam Books

Cranberry Bliss Bar is a registered Trademark of the Starbucks Corporation

Friedrichs, E. (2017, January 16th) *Food Choices Aren't Moral Issues – Here's How to Stop Making Kids Think They Are*. Retrieved from: http://everydayfeminism.com/2017/01/teach-kids-food-choices-arent-moral/

García, Nina (2008). *The One Hundred*. New York, NY: HarperCollins Publishers

Gibran, Kahlil (1923). *The Prophet*. New York, NY: Alfred A. Knopf Publisher

Klein, J. (Head Writer) & McFaul, R. and Powell, D. (Director). (2014). I'm So Bad. Schumer, A. & Klein, J. & Powell, D. (Executive Producer), *Inside Amy Schumer*. New York, New York: Comedy Central.

Poretsky, Golda (2010). *Stop Dieting Now: 25 Reasons To Stop, 25 Ways To Heal.* [Ebook Version] Retrieved from www.amazon.com

Quan, Karen (2015). *Write Like No One is Reading 2* [Ebook Version] Retrieved from www.amazon.com

Smith, Zadie (2006). *On Beauty*. New York, NY: Penguin Group

Turner, Ashley (2017). Retrieved from www.ashleyturner.org

Winfrey, O. (2012) Retrieved from www.goodreads.com

Wolf, Naomi (2002) *The Beauty Myth: How Images of Beauty Are Used Against Women*. New York, NY: HarperCollins Publishers

#######

About the Author

A CALIFORNIA NATIVE, Natalie Carey grew up dancing ballet and performing in musical theater. She began running in college, took up weight lifting while living in Japan, and began pole dancing when she returned to the Bay Area. She is a personal trainer and lives in San Francisco. She believes that women are all capable of feeling beautiful, valuable, and awesome.

Visit her website www.barbellblondie.com to join a community of women advocating positive body image and to find even more resources for your journey towards awesome.

Watch health and positivity in action on her Instagram @barbellblondie

NATALIE CAREY

49195290R00063

Made in the USA
San Bernardino, CA
16 May 2017